A GUIDE TO AUTISM IN THE WORKPLACE

A Guide to Autism in the Workplace
Best Practices for Accommodating Autistic Employees
Dr. Samuel Steinberg

Published by BooxAi

ISBN 978-965-578-049-9

A GUIDE TO AUTISM IN THE WORKPLACE

BEST PRACTICES FOR ACCOMMODATING AUTISTIC EMPLOYEES

DR. SAMUEL STEINBERG

CONTENTS

1

INTRODUCTION TO AUTISM

Autism was first identified in 1911 by a German psychiatrist named Eugen Bleuler. Bleuler categorized autism as a symptom of severe schizophrenia. In the 1960s, the word 'Autism' took a major shift and by the 1980s, autism finally received a separate and distinct diagnosis from schizophrenia.

To this day, people continue to challenge the basic understanding of autism.

While the majority of available resources are geared towards helping children navigate autism, a much smaller amount of resources has been used to help adults.

One major area that needs attention is autism in the workplace.

Statistics vary, but they all have one thing in common:

The majority of people with autism do not have full-time positions, despite many of them wanting to be employed.

In fact, it's reported that nearly 42% of young adults on the spectrum never worked for pay in their early 20s.

Even more surprising, the unemployment rate for people with autism is *higher than it is for any other disability group.*

In this book, we will further dive into what autism spectrum disorder is, why employment can be difficult for people on the spectrum, and what workplaces can do to achieve greater success with employees on the spectrum.

2

WHAT IS AUTISM SPECTRUM DISORDER?

Autism is a developmental disability that can affect many different areas of a person's life, from childhood to adulthood.

Some of those areas include social skills, repetitive behavior, speech, sensory difficulties, unusual abilities, and nonverbal communication.

In the early 1990s, psychiatrists began recognizing that autism presented in many different forms ranging from mild to severe. They started categorizing autistic traits on a spectrum, rather than a finite set of symptoms.

That's why today you'll hear the words "on the spectrum" and why it's called autism spectrum disorder, or ASD for short.

Some people describe autism as having a brain that works with a different operating system than other people. It would be similar to comparing an Apple computer to a Microsoft computer.

FREQUENTLY ASKED QUESTIONS ABOUT AUTISM

1. ***How many people have autism?*** According to the CDC, today 1 in 54 children are diagnosed with autism spectrum disorder (ASD), a number which has increased steadily over recent decades. This number may be underreported as girls are often diagnosed late or never at all.

2. ***What is neurodiversity or neurodivergent?*** Being neurodivergent means having a brain that functions differently than the dominant societal standards of "normal."Autism falls under the term "neurodiverse" which also includes people with ADHD, dyslexia, and Tourette syndrome.

3. ***What is neurotypical?*** Neurotypical describes people who are not autistic and who developed intellectually and cognitively in a "typical" way.

4. ***Are all autistic people the same?*** No, autism has a wide range of symptoms and does not present the same in every person. **No two people on the spectrum are exactly alike in symptoms or personalities.**

5. ***What is Asperger's Syndrome?*** Asperger's Syndrome previously referred to people with autism who might be considered "high functioning." As of 2013, Asperger's is no longer considered a distinct diagnosis. It's now under the umbrella of autism spectrum disorder. Some people still use this term to refer to people with "mild" autism, but it's largely not used in the mental health field today.

6. ***What are the causes of ASD?*** There are some potentially unknown causes of ASD, but the

environment, genetics, and biological factors can all play a role. Some risk factors include being born to older parents, having low birth weight, or having immediate family members with autism.

7. ***What are the signs and symptoms of ASD?*** People on the autism spectrum exhibit signs and symptoms differently. Some experience very severe symptoms, while others may only have mild symptoms. Some may have both mild and severe symptoms. Most people on the spectrum share these traits of autism.

- Social communication challenges
- Restricted, repetitive behaviors

8. What does ASD look like in adulthood?

Adults with ASD range from mild to severe with symptoms, but most have communication and behavior challenges.

Some symptoms include:

- Trouble interpreting facial expression
- Difficulty understanding sarcasm or idioms -- taking language very literally
- Anxiety about social situations
- Struggle to make and maintain friendships
- May come across as blunt or rude
- Prefer to have a routine and may become anxious when routines change
- Avoid eye contact
- Difficulty expressing feelings
- Strong special interest in one or two areas
- Unusual interests
- Clumsiness

- Prefer to work alone towards a goal as opposed to working in a group
- Involuntary noises such as throat clearing
- Engage in repetitive behaviors such as hand flapping, fidgeting, body rocking, repeating certain phrases
- Sensory issues and sensitivity to things like light, sound, or smells

9. Does ASD look the same in men and women? No, women are often diagnosed later in life than men or not at all because their symptoms can be different. These are some ways that women may show autism differently than men:

- May have less severe symptoms than men
- May have an interest in things that may be typical for girls such as fashion or appearance, but with much more intensity
- Camouflaging or "hiding" their autism. Some neurodivergent women will force themselves to make eye contact, prepare conversations ahead of time, and mimic social behaviors, expressions, or gestures.

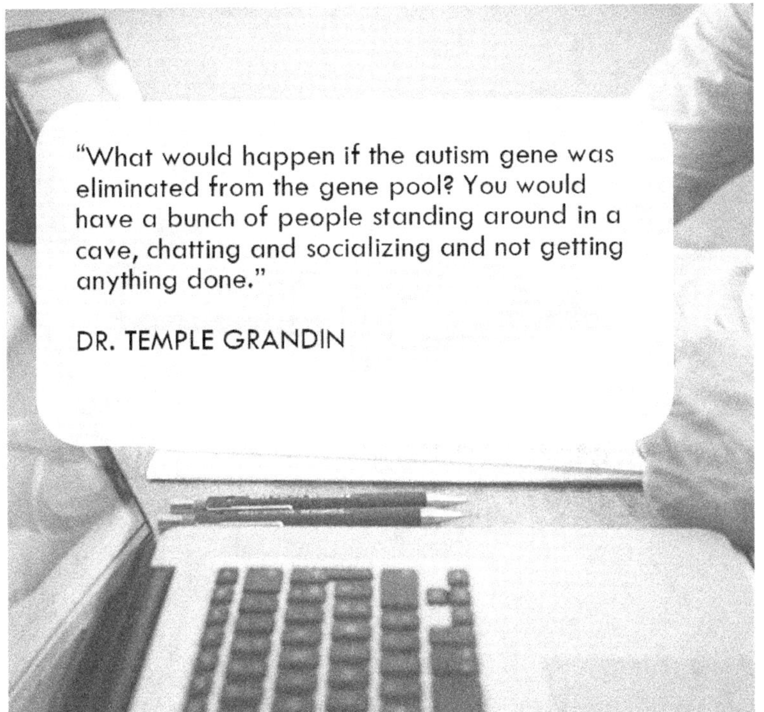
"What would happen if the autism gene was eliminated from the gene pool? You would have a bunch of people standing around in a cave, chatting and socializing and not getting anything done."

DR. TEMPLE GRANDIN

3

WHY DO PEOPLE WITH ASD STRUGGLE TO GET HIRED AND KEEP JOBS?

According to a research presented by the United Kingdom's Autistic Society (NAS), the unemployment rate for people on the spectrum is very high.

They surveyed 2,000 autistic adults and discovered that only 16% were employed full-time. Even more revealing is that 77% of those unemployed *wanted* to work.

Though many people with autism spend their lives trying to fit into society, schools, workplaces, and businesses can also work towards **making it easier for them to be themselves.**

A DIFFERENT WAY OF LOOKING AT DISABILITY

In a TEDx called *Everything You Know About Autism is Wrong,* speaker Jac den Houting explored a different way of looking at autism. Instead of blaming the autistic person for not fitting into a neurotypical (meaning non-autistic) world, it's important to understand that our society and environment aren't working for them.

Here is her definition of disability as it relates to autism:

Disability happens when a person's environment doesn't cater to their individual characteristics. In the social model, we don't refer to people with a disability. Disability isn't something that I carry around like luggage. Instead, we use the word disabled as a verb. Disability is something that is being done to me. I'm actively being disabled by the society around me. The shopping mall is designed in a way that doesn't cater to my needs.

Simply put, many work environments don't take into consideration the unique needs of people with autism.

That doesn't mean that people on the spectrum can't learn new things or strive to understand their neurotypical colleagues. But they don't have to be the only ones adapting. Others around them can adapt as well.

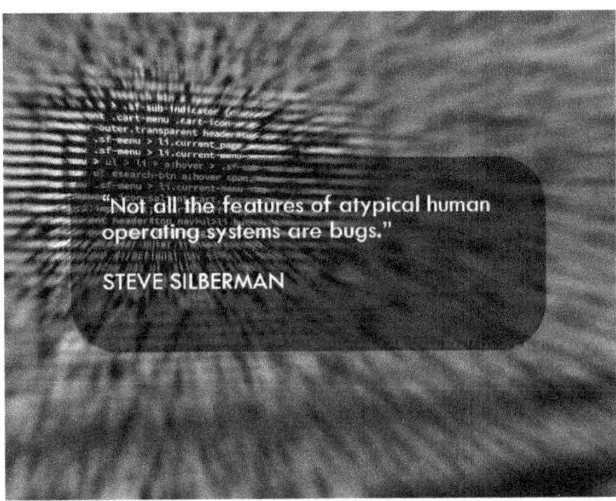

4

WHY HIRE SOMEONE ON THE AUTISM SPECTRUM?

Many employers are looking for the bottom line -- can they hire someone who will complete the job? For many on the spectrum, the answer is yes, but it may require some adjustments.

Today, companies are beginning to look at neurodiversity in a different light.

In fact, many businesses are realizing that neurodiversity can be a real benefit.

According to *Forbes* magazine, "Social difficulties are one of the hallmarks of ASD, making it hard for those with ASD to make it through a traditional hiring process. Roughly 60% of people with ASD have average or above average intelligence, yet 85% are unemployed."

In an article published by *Harvard Business Review* called *"Neurodiversity as a Competitive Advantage"*, authors Robert D. Austin and Gary P. Pisano write, "Because neurodiverse people are wired differently from "neurotypical" people, they may bring new perspectives to a company's efforts to create or recognize value."

HOW DOES NEURODIVERSITY HELP COMPANIES?

Over the past few decades, research has suggested that companies with a diverse workforce perform better. They experience lower turnover rates, higher productivity and produce more creative solutions.

The same is true for neurodiversity. People on the spectrum may not excel in traditional workplace goals like teamwork, communication skills, or networking. However, they provide different skills that are highly beneficial to businesses.

Some traits that many ASD people share are **trustworthiness, reliability, attention to detail, focused effort, innovation, and logical thinking.** They also tend to follow the rules and regulations very closely when they're explained well.

WHAT JOBS ARE A GOOD MATCH FOR PEOPLE WITH AUTISM?

While not every field or every job is made for people with autism, there are loads of places where they have the ability to thrive.

Below are some possible jobs that would work well for people with autism.

Of course, this isn't an exhaustive list of jobs. Personality, ability, and interest will play a huge factor in finding the right job. Just with neurotypical people, there's no single perfect job for all neurodiverse people.

Tech Jobs

Some people with ASD are a natural fit in the tech world. With a global "tech talent gap," many big-name tech companies are seeking autistic employees who are well suited for those types of jobs.

Some of the jobs include:

- Computer animation
- Video game designer
- Software developer
- UI or UX designers
- Social media marketer
- Website designer
- Computer repair
- Computer programming
- Coding

Non-tech Jobs For People With ASD

Not every person on the spectrum will have an interest or ability to thrive in the tech world. Technology isn't the only field that can benefit from people with ASD.

Other jobs that may be a good fit are:

- Marketing
- Automobile mechanic
- Engineering
- Academia
- Library science
- Drafting
- Commercial art
- Photography

- Laboratory technician
- Paramedic or EMT
- Artisan or maker
- Building maintenance
- Factory maintenance
- Accounting
- Journalism
- Copy editor
- Telemarketing
- Statistician
- Physicist
- Mathematician
- Data entry
- Reshelving library books
- Factory assembly work
- Plant care
- Restocking shelves
- Lawn and garden work
- Recycling plant
- Taxi driver
- Animal trainer

COMPANIES WITH NEURODIVERSE HIRING PRACTICES

Over recent years, companies have been tapping into the inherent benefit of a diverse workforce.

Here is a list of some of those companies who see ASD as a notable advantage and are actively hiring people on the spectrum:

- **SAP,** a German IT and software corporation, started an Autism at Work program in 2013 to actively recruit people on the spectrum. Their goal was not only to recruit neurodiverse employees but also to create a welcoming work environment. They report a 90% retention rate of employees.
- **Microsoft** launched an Autism Program shortly after SAP to specifically hire individuals with autism.
- **J.P. Morgan**, an investment bank, started an Autism at Work program in 2015.
- **Hewlett Packard** began the DXC Dandelion Program to hire people on the spectrum to work in IT.
- **Freddie Mac** started an Autism Internship Program in 2012.
- **Ernst & Young** launched a neurodiversity program in 2016.
- **Goldman Sachs** began its Neurodiversity Hiring Initiative in 2019.
- **Daivergent** provides data labeling and annotation services and employs people who are neurodivergent. This company helps other companies connect with neurodivergent applicants.
- **Specialisterne** is a non-profit social enterprise that helps companies, universities, and schools work better with a neurodiverse community. Harvard Business School called them the "gold standard of neurodiversity."

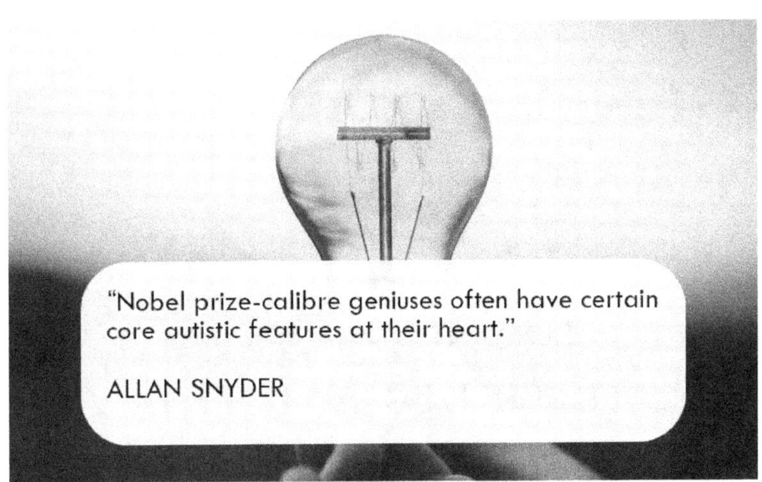
"Nobel prize-calibre geniuses often have certain
core autistic features at their heart."

ALLAN SNYDER

5
AUTISM SPECTRUM DISORDER AND THE INTERVIEWING PROCESS

While there are many benefits to hiring people with autism, the interviewing process can often be a stopping block.

Many people with autism report that they aren't able to get a job because they don't interview well.

If they don't interview well, it can be difficult for the employer to tell if they're capable of performing the job tasks that they're interviewing for, much less be able to tell that they might indeed excel at the job better than other interviewees.

In an interview with *Market Watch,* several autistic people shared their struggles:

- Dylan Mah graduated with a degree in cellular microbiology in 2015. At the time the article was written in 2019, he was still seeking employment as a lab technician or research assistant.

- He explained that the interview process was the part that was most stressful. He said, "The most difficult part is, honestly, just talking to people. It makes me anxious to put myself out there. I really do not like rejection, but I have been, repeatedly."
- Another interviewee shared this opinion. He said, "It can be difficult to interview because it's hard to come off as natural and professional at the same time. I have a degree in library science. I know how the Dewey decimal system works, but it can be hard for me to sell that to an employer."

In many cases, people on the spectrum struggle to get through interviews, let alone to be hired, despite being college-educated and knowledgeable about the job.

So, what can be done to make the interviewing process easier for people with ASD? We'll explore some options below that can help alleviate some of the stress and difficulty with interviews.

HOW TO MAKE MODIFICATIONS FOR SUCCESSFULLY INTERVIEWING PEOPLE WITH ASD

In some cases, simple changes to the way employers interview can make a huge difference in the lives of people with autism.

Many people with ASD are so overwhelmed with anxiety at the thought of an interview that they are unable to perform under the stress of it.

Here are some ways to make this process go more smoothly for everyone involved:

1. **Limit the number of people interviewing the applicant.** A panel of interviewers can cause anyone to be anxious, but for people with ASD, it could be completely debilitating. Having only one or two people conducting an interview is one way to limit concerns.

2. **Do interviews over the phone.** Having an interview over the phone instead of in-person can be another way to relieve stress.

3. **Provide interview questions ahead of time.** Giving the interviewee a list of questions to review before the interview can be highly beneficial for people with ASD.

4. **Keep the interview room as free from distractions as possible.** Find a place to interview the applicant that will not have a lot of noise or visual input. For example, a coffee shop or restaurant would not be an easy place for an autistic person to answer interview questions.

5. **Think about the way questions are worded.** One of the hallmark signs of autism is taking things spoken very literally. If a question could be misinterpreted, consider asking it a different way.

6. **Rethink the interview process entirely.** In some cases, it may make more sense to let a person show you if they can complete a task rather than make it through a traditional interview. For instance, the bank J.P. Morgan uses pymetric games to assess the potential strengths of candidates.

- A skills test may be a better way to assess ability, and this could potentially be finished at home so as to not have the added stress of someone watching the performance.

7. **Look for different strengths.** In many cases, people on the autism spectrum don't perform well in interviews because they don't have the strengths typically looked for in an interview.

- Things like being a team player or great communication skills don't highlight what an autistic person can add to a company.
- Look again and ask if those ideas of what makes a good employee are actually essential to the job they're applying for.

6

HOW TO CREATE A PRODUCTIVE ENVIRONMENT FOR AN AUTISTIC EMPLOYEE

Once an autistic person makes it past the interview process, they may still struggle.

A lot of people on the spectrum report that they were hired to a job and fired without really knowing why. They must have made a big mistake somewhere, but they don't know what it was.

Changing the way that companies accommodate their neuro-diverse employees will go a long way in reducing these kinds of problems.

Companies like SAP and Microsoft, who have intentionally added people on the spectrum to their workforce and have included new accommodations for their ASD employees, have seen very high retention rates -- sometimes as high as 90%.

Quinn, an autistic man who was diagnosed in his teenage years, created a video series called Autistamatic to help

people with autism. In a video entitled *Autism & Society --
Accommodations at Work,* he states,

> Understanding and meeting the basic needs of neurodiver-
> gent people...goes a long way towards making our lives
> more comfortable and carries the jewel business benefits of
> increasing our productivity and reducing downtime. When a
> neurodivergent person works in a field they find stimulating
> and matched to their skill set, they can often outperform
> their neurotypical colleagues. So ensuring they're given the
> opportunity to flourish helps both the employee and the
> employer.

In this section, we'll explore the different ways that companies can accommodate their autistic employees and establish a
more productive workplace.

AMERICAN DISABILITY ACT

In many countries in the world, there are already laws in place
that support people with disabilities. In America, this law is
called the American Disability Act (ADA), and many people
with ASD are included in its protections.

The ADA was established in 1990 and it prohibits discrimina-
tion against people with disabilities.

**It guarantees that people in the US with disabilities have
equal opportunities in areas like public accommodations,
transportation, and employment.**

So long as a potential employee can perform the essential
tasks of a job, they must be considered for the position, and

they can't be turned away simply because they have a disability.

What are Reasonable Accommodations?

You may have heard the term "reasonable accommodations" when referring to individuals with disabilities in the workforce. But what exactly does that mean?

The ADA defines it like this:

A reasonable accommodation is any change to the application or hiring process, to the job, to the way the job is done, or the work environment that allows a person with a disability who is qualified for the job to perform the essential functions of that job and enjoy equal employment opportunities. Accommodations are considered "reasonable" if they do not create an undue hardship or a direct threat.

Some of those accommodations might include:

- A change in job tasks
- Improving accessibility to work (providing a wheelchair ramp, for example)
- Allowing a flexible work schedule
- Change presentation methods for tests or training materials

According to Job Accommodation Network (JAN), a group that helps guide businesses to accommodate people with disabilities, **58% of accommodations cost nothing to employers.**

Of the remaining 42% of costs, 37% said the accommodation was a one-time cost.

For companies spending money to help their employees with disabilities, **tax incentives may be available to help offset any costs.**

JAN also reported, "Employers who had implemented accommodations...were asked to rank the effectiveness of the accommodations on a scale of 1 to 5, with 5 being extremely effective. Of the 877 respondings, the majority (74%) reported the accommodations were either very effective or extremely effective."

COMMUNICATION WITH YOUR ASD EMPLOYEE

For most employee/employer relationships, communication is key. It is no less so with people with autism. Communication might look a little different, but it's still essential.

These are a few ways to help autistic employees perform more effectively in communication:

1. **Let your ASD employees know exactly what you need.** Be very clear and specific about necessary tasks. Daily lists that order tasks by priority can be a really helpful tool.
2. **Ask your employees what they need.** Many ASD employees will have an idea of what works best for them, especially if they were diagnosed in childhood. Give them an opportunity to tell you what accommodations suit them. Not every person on the spectrum will require the same adjustments.

3. **Send emails about expectations.** It's a good idea to send emails to autistic employees to let them know what you want them to do. This will give them something to refer back to and give each of you a paper trail for expectations.

4. **Speak in plain language.** Most people on the spectrum take things very literally. This means you may have to choose your words more carefully when you explain a task. Metaphors, idioms, and expressions may be confusing to your employee, but the same is true for directions that are vague or ambiguous.

5. **Define expectations that may seem obvious.** You may take some workplace expectations for granted, but it may not be so for your autistic employee. For example, if you expect employees to dress in business casual, tell them exactly the type of clothing you would like them to wear.

6. **Give a definition of the rules.** Most autistic people want to follow the rules and will do so when they understand what they are. Ensure that you detail the rules for them, so they know what you want.

SENSORY ISSUES

One of the major signs of autism is sensory issues. This means the body either overreacts or underreacts to a stimulus.

A sensory issue may manifest as someone who can't stand the feeling of tags on their shirts or someone who gets anxious or upset when they're around distracting sounds. However, those who are hyposensitive may actually prefer noises or additional stimuli to feel calm.

Many people on the spectrum are a mix of both.

As mentioned before, the best way to know what will help your autistic employee is by asking them. They will be the best at identifying their needs.

Consider these accommodations that an ASD employee might need:

1. **A private place to work.** Some autistic employees will appreciate a private place to work where they can control things like light and noise.
2. **Switch out the lights.** Many people with autism are sensitive to fluorescent lights. The lights sometimes flicker and create a high-pitched buzzing sound that can trigger people with autism. These fluorescent lights can be switched with natural lighting and or natural spectrum LED lighting.
3. **Blinds for the windows.** If your employee is next to a window, you can provide blinds so they can control how much light comes through.
4. **Noise-canceling headphones.** Employees may like to use noise-cancellation headphones if sounds are too intrusive or distracting.
5. **Music on headphones.** Some ASD employees may need extra sensory input. Listening to music on headphones could be a helpful solution.
6. **Sensitivity from other employees.** When feasible, other employees may be able to help out their autistic colleagues. For instance, encouraging other employees to avoid eating strong-smelling foods outside of the rest areas could be helpful.

7. **Sensory breaks.** Your autistic employee may need small breaks so they can have a break from too many stimuli or seek extra stimuli when necessary.

SOCIAL ACCOMMODATIONS

The social aspect of employment is often the most difficult for people with autism. A simple group meeting may be enough to cause extreme anxiety for someone on the spectrum.

Some people on the spectrum do something called "masking" or "camouflaging." This essentially means that they do their best to pretend they're not autistic in order to fit in. Masking is extremely draining and can make a person feel exhausted at work. It can also distract them from the job they're being paid for.

These are some ways to help an ASD employee feel more socially comfortable at work:

- **Give them the option to not participate.** Allow your employee to make the decision, but things like team-building activities or team-based training may be too much for your autistic employee.
- **Offer less pressure to attend group briefings.** If it isn't totally necessary for an employee to attend a group meeting, give them the option of opting out.

Give them the opportunity to send ideas via email before the meeting.

Send them a recap email after the meeting.

Do the presentation to a camera if you need them to see it.

- **Make parties optional.** Christmas parties, summer events, and retreats may not be beneficial to your ASD employee. Always make them feel welcome to come but avoid making it a requirement.
- **Work closely with HR.** Have a key person in HR that can help your autistic employee. Have someone trained to understand autism that your employee can reach out to when they have a challenge at work.

DAILY SCHEDULE

People with ASD often have the ability to hyper-focus on a project and be extremely productive. A predictable work environment can greatly enhance their ability to perform.

These are some ways to help your employee on a daily schedule:

1. **Routine is key.** Having a routine is an effective way to reduce stress and make expectations clear for an ASD employee.
2. **Give time to transition between tasks.** Some people on the spectrum struggle to quickly transition between tasks. Give them time to switch from one task to another.
3. **Shorter breaks throughout the day.** Give employees time to take short breaks throughout the day when necessary. This may work better than one long break in the middle of the day or may be in addition to a normal lunch break.

TRAINING FOR NEUROTYPICAL EMPLOYEES

Another reason that people with autism don't perform well in the workplace is because of workplace bullying. It may not seem likely, but workplace bullying is a real thing for people with autism. This isn't just in high school or college -- this is in adult life.

One way to combat that is to provide sensitivity training to neurotypical employees.

Inclusive training might include:

- Definition of autism
- Why neurodiversity matters
- Understanding differences
- Awareness training
- Ways to communicate more effectively
- How to practice inclusive hiring
- How to manage neurodiverse employees
- Support for neurodiverse employees or colleagues

ADDITIONAL ACCOMMODATIONS

There are also other accommodations that may help your ASD employees function more productively at work.

These ideas include:

1. **Pay by the job.** Some autistic people would prefer to be paid by the job rather than by the hour. When paid by the hour, they sometimes struggle to see an end game. Getting paid for a finished product is a good incentive to keep working.

2. **Offer incentives.** If it's not possible to be paid per project, then offering weekly or monthly goals with incentives may also work well.

3. **Use color-coded systems.** Using a color-coded system often helps students understand expectations in school, but it can also be used in the workplace. It could also be a helpful advantage to neurotypical employees as well.

4. **Use video modeling.** As employees are learning a new task, it's often helpful to use video modeling. It can break down job tasks into simple to follow steps.

Consider Letting Employees Work From Home

Since the height of Covid-19, many companies have been redefining what the workplace looks like. While a typical job may have been a 9-5 in an office setting, today many employees are now able to work from home.

Working from home can be a real advantage for many who are on the autism spectrum.

If working remotely, the person with autism will be able to control sensory things like light, sounds, and smells. They can also manage their own schedule and avoid navigating uncomfortable social interactions.

Not all jobs can be done remotely, but this could be an excellent option for many office jobs.

"Do not fear people with Autism,
embrace them, Do not spite people
with Autism unite them, Do not deny
people with Autism accept them for
then their abilities will shine"

PAUL ISAACS

7
READY TO CELEBRATE A DIVERSE WORKFORCE?

Whether you're thinking about adding some diversity to your workforce or you want to make a more productive environment for your current employees, a good way to start is with knowledge.

This book has outlined what autism is and some great starting points for accommodating an employee with an autism spectrum disorder. **Small adjustments in the way the workplace functions can lead to incredible benefits for you and your employees.**

Once you know more about what it's like to live in the world of autism, don't be afraid to reach out to your autistic employees. This gesture on your part will go a long way in meeting the needs of a community that is often overlooked or disregarded.

Being different can be a true asset to your business, and there's a large group of people willing and ready to join the workforce. Now is a great time to tap into this group of people and set them up with a safe and comfortable place to work.

ABOUT THE AUTHOR

Dr. Samuel Samtosha Steinberg has a doctorate in Metaphysics, is a special education teacher, a Yoga Alliance certified 500 E-RYT yoga teacher and educator and a meditation consultant to mental health practitioners and pain support groups as well as a relaxation teacher. He is the author of "Meditation For People Who Can't Meditate" and "Free Bird", a children's book about freedom. He also authored "Parents Guide to Helping a Child With Learning Disabilities", and "Anxiety, Depression & Panic Attacks."